PLANT BLOSSOMS

David M. Schwartz *is an award-winning author of children's books, on a wide variety of topics, loved by* children around the world. *Dwight Kuhn's* scientific expertise and artful eye work together with the *camera to capture the awesome wonder of the natural world.*

For a free color catalog describing Gareth Stevens Publishing's list of high-quality books and multimedia programs, call 1-800-542-2595 (USA) or 1-800-461-9120 (Canada). Gareth Stevens Publishing's Fax: (414) 225-0377.

Library of Congress Cataloging-in-Publication Data

Schwartz, David M.
    Plant blossoms / by David M. Schwartz; photographs by Dwight Kuhn.
      p. cm. — (Look once, look again)
    Includes bibliographical references and index.
    Summary: Introduces, in simple text and photographs, the flowers of apple trees,
cosmos, grasses, dandelions, foxgloves, and pussy willows.
    ISBN 0-8368-2580-2 (lib. bdg.)
    1. Flowers—Juvenile literature. 2. Buds—Juvenile literature. [1. Flowers.
2. Buds.] I. Kuhn, Dwight, ill. II. Title. III. Series: Schwartz, David M. Look once,
look again.
QK653.S425   2000
582.13—dc21   99-047588

This North American edition first published in 2000 by
Gareth Stevens Publishing
1555 North RiverCenter Drive, Suite 201
Milwaukee, Wisconsin 53212 USA

First published in the United States in 1998 by Creative Teaching Press, Inc., P. O. Box 6017, Cypress, California, 90630-0017.

Text © 1998 by David M. Schwartz; photographs © 1998 by Dwight Kuhn. Additional end matter © 2000 by Gareth Stevens, Inc.

Printed in the United States of America

1 2 3 4 5 6 7 8 9 04 03 02 01 00

PLANT BLOSSOMS

by David M. Schwartz

photographs by Dwight Kuhn

A SPRINGBOARDS INTO SCIENCE SERIES

Gareth Stevens Publishing

MILWAUKEE

These red and green
buds will soon open.
Snowy white flowers
will appear.

These are the blossoms, or flowers, of an apple tree. Bees visit the flowers to drink the sweet nectar. They leave behind pollen from other trees. When pollen falls onto an apple blossom, the flower starts to grow into a crisp, tasty apple.

These are the stamens, or male parts, of a flower.

Insects rub against the stamens of cosmos flowers and become covered with pollen. They carry the pollen to other cosmos flowers.

8

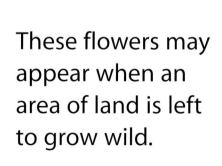

These flowers may
appear when an
area of land is left
to grow wild.

9

Did you know grass plants have flowers? The flowers are small and white. Pollen grains fall from the flowers, and the wind carries them away. If a pollen grain lands on another grass flower, a grass seed will grow.

Up close, this may not look familiar, but you probably know what it is.

A dandelion flower head is made up of many tiny flowers packed tightly together. Each flower head has more than a hundred tiny flowers. These sturdy plants grow everywhere, even in cracks in parking lots!

Do these speckled tubes
look like a glove?

13

Foxglove flowers grow in bunches on long stems. Each flower is like a little tube that could fit over your finger. Maybe that is why it is called a glove.

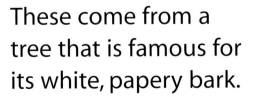

These come from a tree that is famous for its white, papery bark.

15

The flowers of the white birch hang together in clusters. These male catkins will drop their yellow pollen in the wind. If some pollen lands on a female catkin, birch seeds will grow.

These buds
feel like the
fur of a cat.

These are pussy willow buds.
When the buds first open in
spring, they are soft and furry.
When they open even more,
you can see they
are packed with
tiny flowers.

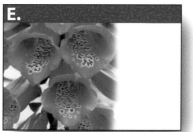

Look closely. Can you name these plants?

LOOK AGAIN

A. Apple tree

B. Cosmos

C. Grass

D. Dandelions

E. Foxglove

F. White birch

G. Pussy willow

How many were you able to identify correctly?

bees: social insects that feed on pollen and nectar.

blossoms: flowers of seed plants.

buds: small swellings on a plant that contain new leaves and flowers.

catkins: tightly packed flowers, without petals, produced by many types of trees.

cluster: similar types of objects that are grouped together.

flower: the seed-producing blossom of a plant.

grains: small, hard particles.

grass plants: plants that have jointed stems, thin leaves, and flowers. The grass family contains about nine thousand species.

insects: small, segmented, invertebrate animals. They each have a well-defined thorax, head, and abdomen. They also each have six legs. Many adults have wings.

nectar: a sugary liquid produced by flowers to attract insects and other animals.

pollen: the powderlike, male cells produced by flowers. Pollen grains fertilize the female parts of the flowers.

seeds: the fertilized, ripened ovules of flowering plants that produce new plants.

stamen: the structure in a flower that produces pollen.

stems: slender stalks that support flowers and the plant.

ACTIVITIES

Powers of Observation

Look at a flower, studying every part of it. Then, close your eyes. What color is the flower? How tall and wide is it? How many petals does it have? What is the shape of its leaves? Are there any seeds? Open your eyes. Are you a good observer? Make a color drawing of the flower. Try again with another flower to see if your powers of observation improve.

They're Everywhere

The next time you take a trip, notice all the wildflowers along the roadside. North America has over forty national parks where wildflowers are conserved. Some state parks are also wildflower sanctuaries. If you can, visit a national or state park, and be sure to take a field guide of flowers along with you. There is probably one available at the library.

Plants, Plants, Plants

Visit your local garden center to see all the varieties of flowers and vegetables on display. The small plants are started from seed during the winter. Conditions are ideal for them in a heated greenhouse. In early spring, plant some flower or vegetable seeds of your own in a milk carton inside the house. When temperatures become warm enough in your area, plant the seedlings outside.

Sponge Gardening

Soak a sponge in water, and put it on a plate. Sprinkle grass seed on top of the sponge. Cover the entire plate (with the sponge on it) tightly with plastic wrap. Put the plate in the sun, and keep the sponge wet. Remove the plastic wrap when grass appears. What do seeds require in order to grow?

More Books to Read

Flowers. David Burnie (Eyewitness Explorers)

Flowers, Trees, and Fruits. Sally Morgan (Kingfisher)

Into the Woods: A Woodland Scrapbook. Loretta Krupinski (HarperCollins)

The Nature and Science of Flowers. Exploring the Science of Nature (series). Jane Burton and Kim Taylor (Gareth Stevens)

The Sunflower Family. Cherie Winner (Carolrhoda)

Wildflowers Around the World. Elaine Landay (Watts)

Videos

The Children's Garden Project. (Video 11)

Flowers, Plants, and Trees. (Moonbeam)

The Magic School Bus: Goes to Seed. (Warner Vision)

Web Sites

www.vg.com

members.xoom.com/beebuzz/bee.htm

Some web sites stay current longer than others. For further web sites, use your search engines to locate the following topics: *bees, flowers, gardens, grasses, insects, nectar, pollen,* and *trees.*

INDEX